Trees

Jennifer Howse

WEIGL PUBLISHERS INC.
"Creating Inspired Learning"
www.weigl.com

Published by Weigl Publishers Inc.
350 5th Avenue, 59th Floor
New York, NY 10118
Website: www.weigl.com

Library of Congress Cataloging-in-Publication Data

Howse, Jennifer.
Trees : world of wonder : watch them grow / Jennifer Howse.
p. cm.
ISBN 978-1-60596-916-9 (hard cover : alk. paper) -- ISBN 978-1-60596-917-6 (soft cover : alk. paper)
-- ISBN 978-1-60596-918-3 (e-book)
1. Trees--Juvenile literature. I. Title.
QK475.8.H69 2010
582.16--dc22
2009052098

Printed in the United States of America in North Mankato, Minnesota
1 2 3 4 5 6 7 8 9 0 14 13 12 11 10

042010
WEP264000

Editor: Heather C. Hudak
Design: Terry Paulhus

Weigl acknowledges Getty Images as its primary image supplier for this title.

CONTENTS

What is a Tree?

Have you ever sat under a tree on a hot day? Trees provide shade from the Sun's rays. They also offer shelter and food for animals. There are many types of trees. They can be found all over the world.

Like all living things, trees have a life cycle. They begin as a seed, **sprout** from the ground, and make more trees.

Trees have three main parts. The trunk supports the tree. Branches grow up and out from the trunk. Roots hold the tree in place.

5

Spreading Seeds

Have you ever planted a seed in a garden? Most trees start life as a seed. The seed comes from a **mature** tree. Most tree seeds are in some type of case, or coat. Nutshells, cones, fruit, and flowers are seed coats. They protect the seed inside.

Wind blows seed coats from trees. This spreads the seeds over a large area. Birds and animals eat seed coats and spread them through their droppings.

Coconut palm tree seeds are inside coconuts. Ocean waves carry them to new places.

Taking Root

What do you need to become big and strong? Like you, seeds need water to help them grow. They need soil that is filled with **nutrients** and air that is a certain temperature. If a seed has these things, it can grow.

First, the seed must split open. One way to do this is for it to soak up water. This causes the seed to **swell**. Then, the seed sends a **shoot** into the soil. This will become the main root. After, the seed starts to sprout aboveground.

Banyan tree roots look like **pillars**. They hang from branches aboveground.

Up From the Ground

Did you know that even the tallest trees start life as a tiny sprout? The first sprout to pop up from the soil is the growing tip. The seed coat is on the tip.

At first, the sprout is folded. As it unfolds, its coat blows away. Over time, the tip grows taller. It also makes small leaves.

Growing Strong

Have you ever tried to climb a tree? Did you wonder how it grew so tall and strong? Trees grow very fast for their first few years of life. There is new growth above and below the ground.

Over time, the roots grow thicker and stronger. They also grow deeper into the ground. Twigs sprout out from the trunk to make new branches. The trunk of the tree grows wider, taller, and stronger. The **crown** forms buds on the tips of branches. Buds also form on the tip of the trunk.

Standing Tall

What age will you be when you are full grown? In most cases, people stop growing by 20 years of age. Trees never stop growing.

Trees are mature when they first start to bloom. The crown of a mature tree is round when filled with leaves. The trunk is tough and hard. Mature tree roots are very thick. They can reach deep into the ground.

The roots take in nutrients and water to feed the tree. This food travels through the whole tree.

Tree Types

Did you know that trees come in all shapes and sizes? There are many types of trees. Each type looks different.

Some trees lose their leaves in fall. Birch, oak, aspen, and poplar are examples. They grow new leaves in spring. This allows the trees to use less energy in winter. Fewer branches break from heavy snow and ice piling on them.

The bark of an aspen tree can be eaten.

Long-lasting Leaves

Did you know that not all trees lose their leaves in fall? Some trees keep their green leaves for more than one season. These trees are called evergreens. They have needle-shaped leaves with a waxy coating.

Most evergreens lose their needles after two or three years. Some trees, such as spruce, keep their leaves for as long as eight or nine years. Larch and tamarack lose their leaves every year.

Life Story

Do you like stories? A tree keeps the story of its life inside its trunk. When a tree is chopped down, its rings can be seen inside the trunk. In most cases, each ring shows one year in the tree's life.

Some rings are small. Others are large. The size of the ring shows how much the tree grew each year of its life. Counting all of the rings will tell the age of the tree when it died.

Scientists can tell the age of living trees. The oldest living tree in the world is a Norway spruce in Sweden. It is more than 9,550 years old.

Family Tree

Supplies

construction paper

white glue

leaves

seeds

grass

twigs

crayons or markers

flowers

1. Glue a leaf in the center of the construction paper. The stem should be pointing to the top of the paper.
2. Draw a face at the top of the stem.
3. Give the leaf arms and legs to make it look like a person.
4. Use the flowers, seeds, twigs, and grass to decorate the leaf person.
5. Add color to your picture using the crayons or markers.
6. Repeat steps 1 to 5 to make more members of your leaf family.

Find Out More

To learn more about trees, visit these websites.

Real Trees 4 Kids!
www.realtrees4kids.org

What Tree Is It?
www.oplin.org/tree

Arbor Day Foundation
www.arborday.org/
trees/index.cfm

The Treetures
www.treetures.com

Glossary

crown: top of the tree where leaves and blooms grow

mature: full grown

nutrients: substances that are needed to help growth

pillars: tall structures that are used for support

shoot: new growth

sprout: to spring up and begin to grow

swell: become larger in size

Index